P9-CKZ-573

little book of

Exotic
Cocktails

little book of

Exotic
Cocktails

hamlyn

First published in 2002 by Hamlyn,
a division of Octopus Publishing Group Limited
2–4 Heron Quays, London E14 4JP

British Library Cataloguing-in-Publication Data
A catalogue record for this book is available from the British Library

ISBN 0 600 60806 9

Printed in China

Notes for American readers

The measure that has been used in the recipes is based on a bar measure,
which is 25 ml (1 fl oz). If preferred, a different volume can be used
providing the proportions are kept constant within a drink and suitable
adjustments are made to spoon measurements, where they occur.

Standard level spoon measurements are used in all recipes.
1 tablespoon = one 15 ml spoon
1 teaspoon = one 5 ml spoon
Imperial and metric measurements have been given in some of the recipes.
Use one set of measurements only.

UK	US
caster sugar	granulated sugar
cocktail cherries	maraschino cherries
cocktail stick	toothpick
double cream	heavy cream
drinking chocolate	presweetened cocoa powder
icing sugar	confectioners' sugar
jug	pitcher
lemon rind	lemon peel or zest
single cream	light cream
soda water	club soda

SAFETY NOTE The Department of Health advises that eggs should not be
consumed raw. This book contains recipes made with raw eggs. It is prudent
for more vulnerable people such as pregnant and nursing mothers, invalids,
the elderly, babies and young children to avoid these recipes.

Contents

Introduction

Cocktails are pure escapism. Frivolous and fun, they are the perfect way to entertain with the maximum of style and the minimum of effort. They are quickly put together and instantly transport the drinker from the mundane world of everyday life.

All over the world people have been experimenting with different combinations of drinks, both alcoholic and non-alcoholic, for centuries. The origin of the name 'cocktail' itself is uncertain, although there are several theories, but whatever the origin of the word, the creation of the cocktail can be traced back to the 19th century.

One of the first of the modern cocktails to be recognised was the Martini, whose origins come from an 1862 recipe for Martinez. This drink was created by 'Professor' Jerry Thomas, bartender at the old Occidental Hotel in San Francisco, for a gold miner returning to his home in Martinez, a town 40 miles to the east. By 1900 the Martini was known across the USA and had even spread to Europe. Around this time a growing list of basic cocktails emerged and steadily gained popularity. Other classic recipes that originated in the 19th century are the Daiquiri, the Mint-Julep and the Manhattan.

The cocktail was given a boost when the Prohibition laws were brought into force in the USA in 1920, making the manufacture or sale of intoxicating liquor illegal. This led to a healthy black market, with bootleggers such as Al Capone distributing moonshine nationwide. The quality of some of this moonshine was rather dubious and cocktails became very popular in the illegal bars and clubs that sprang up at the time, as a means of disguising its raw taste. Many of the classic cocktails we know today were invented during this period, such as the Bloody Mary and the Zombie.

Since then there have been numerous cocktail revivals and new drinks, such as the Pina Colada from the eighties and the B52 from the nineties, have been to be added to the ever-growing repertoire of recipes.

This book provides a selection of the most colourful, unusual and exotic of these cocktails. Chapter One presents eye-catching and colourful drinks, such as the Sapphire Martini, the Silk Stocking and the Snapdragon. Chapter Two offers a range of drinks with unusual combinations of ingredients, including the Knockout, the Shanghai and the Maracuja. Chapter Three gathers together a range of cocktails with exotic associations, from the tropical Singapore Sling to the sublime Paradise. Finally, Chapter Four suggests a wide range of cocktails for parties, with alcoholic and alcohol-free drinks that are guaranteed to delight your guests.

Sugar Syrup

This may be used instead of sugar to sweeten cocktails and give them more body. It can be bought, but is simple to make at home.

Put 4 tablespoons of caster sugar and 4 tablespoons of water in a small saucepan and stir over a low heat until the sugar has dissolved. Bring to the boil and boil, without stirring, for 1–2 minutes. Sugar syrup may be stored in a sterilized bottle in the refrigerator for up to 2 months.

7

Colourful & Striking

Sapphire Martini

4 ice cubes
2 measures gin
½ measure blue Curaçao
1 red or blue cocktail
    cherry (optional)

**Although blue Curaçao
gives this drink its stunning
colour, it is an orange
flavoured liqueur.**

Put the ice cubes into a cocktail
shaker. Pour in the gin and blue
Curaçao. Shake well to mix.
Strain into a cocktail glass and
carefully drop in a cocktail cherry,
if using.

Serves 1

Pousse Café

½ measure Grenadine
½ measure Maraschino
½ measure crème de
   violette
½ measure Chartreuse
½ measure brandy

Maraschino is a colourless liqueur from Italy made with sour maraschino cherries and their crushed kernels.

Carefully pour each of the ingredients in turn into a tumbler or highball glass to form separate layers. The effect should be like a rainbow of distinct colours.

Serves 1

Cobalt Margarita

1 lime wedge
fine sea salt
1¼ measures tequila
2 teaspoons Cointreau
½ measure blue Curaçao
¾ measure fresh
    lime juice
¾ measure fresh
    grapefruit juice
4–5 ice cubes
lime rind spiral, to
    decorate

Dampen the rim of a chilled cocktail glass with a lime wedge then dip it into fine sea salt. Pour the tequila, Cointreau, blue Curaçao, lime juice and grapefruit juice into a cocktail shaker. Add the ice cubes and shake vigorously for 10 seconds then strain into the cocktail glass. Decorate with a lime rind spiral.

Serves 1

colourful & striking

Tip

To make a citrus spiral, pare the rind from the fruit with a canelle knife or vegetable peeler then wind it tightly round a glass swizzle stick.

13

Silk Stocking

drinking chocolate
   powder
¾ measure tequila
¾ measure white crème
   de cacao
100 ml (3½ fl oz) single
   cream
2 teaspoons grenadine
4–5 ice cubes

Dampen the rim of a chilled
cocktail glass and dip it into the
drinking chocolate powder. Pour
the tequila, white crème de
cacao, cream and grenadine into
a cocktail shaker and add the ice
cubes. Shake vigorously for
10 seconds then strain into the
chilled cocktail glass.

Serves 1

Sea Breeze

6–8 ice cubes

½ measure fresh grapefruit juice

½ measure cranberry juice

1 measure dry vermouth

3 measures gin

lime slice, to decorate

Put 2–3 ice cubes into a mixing glass. Pour the grapefruit juice, cranberry juice, vermouth and gin over the ice then stir gently. Put 4–5 fresh ice cubes into a chilled hurricane glass and strain the drink over the ice. Decorate with a lime slice.

Serves 1

Ritz Fizz

1 dash blue Curaçao
1 dash fresh lemon juice
1 dash Amaretto di
    Saronno
Champagne
lemon rind spiral, to
    decorate

Pour the Curaçao, lemon juice
and Amaretto into a glass and
top up with Champagne. Stir
gently to mix and decorate the
glass with a lemon rind spiral.

Serves 1

East India

4–5 ice cubes
3 drops Angostura bitters
½ measure pineapple
    juice
½ measure blue Curaçao
2 measures brandy
orange rind spiral, to
    decorate

A splash of Angostura bitters enlivens many cocktails. The pink element in pink gin, it was first made in the Venezuelan town of Angostura during the 19th century but is now produced in Trinidad.

Put the ice cubes into a mixing glass. Shake the bitters over the ice and add the pineapple juice, Curaçao and brandy. Stir until frothy, then strain into a chilled cocktail glass. Decorate with an orange rind spiral.

Serves 1

Snapdragon

4–6 ice cubes
2 measures vodka
4 measures green crème
   de menthe
soda water
mint sprigs, to decorate

Fill a highball glass with ice
cubes. Add the vodka and crème
de menthe and stir. Top up
with soda water. Decorate with a
mint sprig.

Serves 1

Tip

The sprigs of a great
many different varieties
of mint, such as
spearmint and
applemint, can be used
in cocktails. Their bright
green leaves are both
attractive and refreshing.

Luigi

4–5 ice cubes
1 measure fresh orange
   juice
1 measure dry vermouth
½ measure Cointreau
1 measure grenadine
2 measures gin
orange slice, to decorate

Put the ice cubes into a mixing glass. Pour the orange juice, vermouth, Cointreau, grenadine and gin over the ice and stir vigorously. Strain into a chilled cocktail glass, decorate with the orange slice and serve.

Serves 1

Port Antonio

½ teaspoon grenadine
4–5 ice cubes
1 measure fresh
    lime juice
3 measures white rum or
    golden rum

to decorate
lime rind
cocktail cherry

Grenadine is a sweet non-alcoholic syrup made from pomegranates, which give it its rich rosy pink colour.

Spoon the grenadine into a chilled cocktail glass. Put the ice cubes into a mixing glass. Pour the lime juice and rum over the ice and stir vigorously, then strain into the cocktail glass. Wrap the lime rind round the cocktail cherry, spear them with a cocktail stick and use to decorate the drink.

Serves 1

colourful & striking

Mockingbird

1¼ measures tequila

¾ measure green crème
de menthe

1¼ measures fresh
lime juice

4–5 ice cubes

lemon rind spiral, to
decorate

Pour the tequila, crème de
menthe and lime juice into a
cocktail shaker. Add the ice
cubes, shake vigorously for about
10 seconds then strain into a
chilled cocktail glass. Decorate
with a lemon rind spiral.

Serves 1

Unusual Combinations

Shanghai

3 ice cubes, crushed
1 measure brandy
½ measure Curaçao
¼ measure Maraschino
2 dashes Angostura
    bitters

to decorate
lemon rind spiral
cocktail cherry

Put the ice cubes into a cocktail shaker and add the brandy, Curaçao, Maraschino and bitters. Shake to mix. Pour into a cocktail glass and decorate with the lemon rind spiral and a cocktail cherry on a cocktail stick.

Serves 1

Corpse Reviver

3 ice cubes, cracked
2 measures brandy
1 measure calvados
1 measure sweet
   vermouth
apple slice, to decorate

Put the ice, brandy, calvados and sweet vermouth into a cocktail shaker and shake until a frost forms on the outside of the shaker. Strain, or pour without straining if desired, into a glass and decorate with an apple slice.

Serves 1

Fifth Avenue

1 measure brown crème
de cacao

1 measure apricot brandy

1 measure cream

Pour the ingredients carefully
in the order given into a straight-
sided liqueur glass so that each
ingredient floats on the
preceding one.

Serves 1

Tip

Crème de cacao is a
chocolate-flavoured
liqueur which comes in
colourless and chocolate-
brown varieties.

Knockout

4–5 ice cubes
1 measure dry vermouth
½ measure white crème
    de menthe
2 measures gin
1 drop pernod
lemon slice, to serve

Crème de menthe is a sweetish mint-flavoured liqueur. It may be green or white, although the flavour remains the same. The white version is used here to blend with the milky colour of the pernod.

Put the ice cubes into a mixing glass. Pour the vermouth, crème de menthe and gin over the ice, stir vigorously, then strain into a chilled old-fashioned glass. Add the pernod and serve with a lemon slice.

Serves 1

Parisien

1 measure brandy
½ measure calvados
1 measure fresh lemon
     juice
sugar syrup (see page 7)
½ measure Poire William
     (pear liqueur)
fruits, to decorate

Fill a tumbler with crushed ice,
add the brandy, calvados, lemon
juice and some sugar syrup to
taste. Pour the Poire William over
the top and decorate with fruits.

Serves 1

Zombie

3 ice cubes, cracked
1 measure dark rum
1 measure white rum
½ measure golden rum
½ measure apricot brandy
juice of ½ lime
2 measures
    unsweetened
    pineapple juice
2 teaspoons powdered
    sugar

to decorate
slice of kiwi fruit
cocktail cherry
pineapple wedge
powdered sugar
    (optional)

Zombies contain all three types of rum – dark, golden and white. The darker rums are aged in charred oak casks while white rums are aged in stainless steel tanks.

Place a tall glass in the freezer so the outside becomes frosted. Put the ice into a cocktail shaker. Add the rums, apricot brandy, lime juice, pineapple juice and sugar. Shake to mix. Pour into the glass without straining. To decorate, spear the slice of kiwi fruit, cherry and pineapple with a cocktail stick and place it across the top of the glass, balanced on the rim. Sprinkle the powdered sugar over the top and serve.

Serves 1

Leo

2–3 ice cubes, crushed
1 measure brandy
1½ measures fresh
    orange juice
½ measure Amaretto di
    Saronno
soda water
1 teaspoon Campari

**Campari is an Italian
aperitif wine with a strong,
bitter taste and bright red
colour.**

Put the ice into a cocktail shaker.
Add the brandy, orange juice and
Amaretto. Shake well. Strain into
a tall glass and add soda water to
taste, and the Campari.

Serves 1

Tip

Amaretto di Saronno is
a liqueur made from
almonds and apricots,
first made in Saronno,
Italy, in the 16th century.

Vodka Sour

4–5 ice cubes
2 measures vodka
½ measure sugar syrup
    (see page 7)
1 egg white
1½ measures fresh
    lemon juice
3 drops Angostura
    bitters, to decorate

Put the ice cubes into a cocktail
shaker, add the vodka, sugar
syrup, egg white and lemon juice
and shake until a frost forms.
Pour without straining into a
cocktail glass and shake 3 drops
of Angostura bitters on the top
to decorate.

Serves 1

Honolulu

4–5 ice cubes
1 measure pineapple
   juice
1 measure fresh lemon
   juice
1 measure fresh orange
   juice
½ teaspoon grenadine
3 measures gin

to decorate
pineapple slice
cocktail cherry

Put the ice cubes into a cocktail shaker. Pour the pineapple, lemon and orange juices, the grenadine and gin over the ice and shake until a frost forms. Strain the drink into a chilled cocktail glass and decorate with the pineapple and cherry.

Serves 1

Caribbean Champagne

1 tablespoon light rum
1 tablespoon crème de
     banane
1 dash Angostura bitters
Champagne

to decorate
banana slice
pineapple slice
cocktail cherry

Pour the rum, crème de banane
and bitters into a chilled
Champagne flute. Top up with
Champagne and stir gently.
Decorate with the banana,
pineapple and cherry, all speared
on a cocktail stick.

Serves 1

Maracuja

1 fresh ripe passion fruit
1¼ measures tequila gold
1 tablespoon Creole
    Shrub
¾ measure fresh lime
    juice
2 teaspoons Cointreau
1 teaspoon passion
    fruit syrup
4–5 ice cubes
physalis (Cape
    gooseberry), to
    decorate

Creole Shrub is a golden-coloured rum, flavoured with orange peel.

Cut the passion fruit in half and scoop the flesh into a cocktail shaker. Add the tequila, Creole Shrub, lime juice, Cointreau, passion fruit syrup and ice cubes and shake vigorously for 10 seconds. Strain through a small fine sieve into a chilled cocktail glass. Decorate with a physalis.

Serves 1

Tip

It is important to use a really ripe passion fruit for this drink.

Cherry Julep

3–4 ice cubes
juice of ½ lemon
1 teaspoon sugar syrup
  (see page 7)
1 teaspoon grenadine
1 measure cherry brandy
1 measure sloe gin
2 measures gin
chopped ice
lemon rind strips, to
  decorate

Put the ice cubes into a cocktail shaker. Pour the lemon juice, sugar syrup, grenadine, cherry brandy, sloe gin and gin over the ice. Fill a highball glass with finely chopped ice. Shake the mixture until a frost forms then strain it and pour into the ice-filled glass. Decorate with lemon rind strips and serve.

Serves 1

Havana Beach

½ lime
2 measures pineapple
    juice
1 measure white rum
1 teaspoon sugar
ginger ale, to top up
lime slice, to decorate

A hurricane glass is so called because it is shaped like a hurricane lamp. It is ideal for long drinks.

Cut the lime into 4 pieces and place in a blender with the pineapple juice, rum and sugar. Blend until smooth. Pour into a hurricane glass or large goblet and top up with ginger ale. Decorate with a slice of lime.

Serves 1

Forest Fruit

1 lime wedge
brown sugar
2 blackberries
2 raspberries
2 teaspoons Chambord
2 teaspoons crème
   de mure
1¼ measures tequila
2 teaspoons Cointreau
1¼ measures fresh
   lemon juice
crushed ice

to decorate
lemon slices
blackberry
raspberry

Chambord is a black raspberry liqueur and crème de mure is a blackberry one.

Dampen the rim of an old-fashioned glass with a lime wedge and dip it into brown sugar. Drop the blackberries and raspberries into the glass and muddle to a pulp with the back of a spoon or a porcelain pestle. Stir in the Chambord and Crème de Mure. Pour in the tequila, Cointreau and lemon juice, fill with crushed ice and stir gently, lifting the muddled berries from the bottom of the glass. Decorate with lemon slices, a blackberry and a raspberry.

Serves 1

Exotic Associations

Tobago Fizz

4–5 ice cubes
juice of ½ lime or lemon
juice of ½ orange
3 measures golden rum
1 measure single cream
½ teaspoon sugar syrup
    (see page 7)
soda water

to decorate
orange slice
strawberry slice

Put the ice cubes into a cocktail shaker. Pour the lime or lemon juice, orange juice, rum, cream and sugar syrup over the ice. Shake until a frost forms, then strain into a goblet. Top with soda water and serve decorated with slices of orange and strawberry speared on a cocktail stick and drink with straws.

Serves 1

Vodka Twister Fizz

exotic associations

4–5 ice cubes
juice of 1 lemon
½ teaspoon sugar syrup
   (see page 7)
1 egg white
3 drops Pernod
3 measures vodka
ginger ale
lime slice, to decorate

Put the ice cubes into a cocktail shaker. Pour the lemon juice, sugar syrup, egg white, Pernod and vodka over the ice and shake until a frost forms. Pour without straining into a highball glass and top up with ginger ale. Stir once or twice and decorate with a lime slice.

Serves 1

Singapore Sling

1–2 cracked ice cubes
1 measure gin
¼ measure cherry brandy
¼ measure Cointreau
juice of ½ lemon
soda water

to decorate
pineapple slice
strawberry
orange slice

Put the ice into a tall glass. Add the gin, cherry brandy, Cointreau and lemon juice. Stir and top up with soda water. Decorate with the pineapple, strawberry and orange speared on a cocktail stick and serve with a straw.

Serves 1

Brandy Egg Sour

3 ice cubes, cracked
1 egg
1 teaspoon caster sugar
3 dashes fresh lemon
 juice
1 measure orange
 Curaçao
1 measure brandy

to decorate
orange slice
cocktail cherry

Put the ice, egg, sugar, lemon juice, Curaçao and brandy into a cocktail shaker and shake well. Strain into a tumbler. Decorate with an orange slice and a cherrry speared on a cocktail stick. Serve with straws.

Serves 1

Gin Tropical

4–6 ice cubes
1½ measures gin
1 measure fresh lemon
    juice
1 measure passion fruit
    juice
½ measure fresh orange
    juice
soda water
orange rind spiral, to
    decorate

Put 2–3 ice cubes into a cocktail
shaker, pour in the gin, lemon
juice, passion fruit juice and
orange juice and shake well.
Put 2–3 fresh ice cubes into an
old-fashioned glass and strain
the cocktail over the ice. Top
up with soda water and stir
gently. Decorate with an orange
rind spiral.

Serves 1

Acapulco

crushed ice
1 measure tequila
1 measure white rum
2 measures
    pineapple juice
1 measure fresh
    grapefruit juice
1 measure coconut milk
pineapple wedge,
    to decorate

Whenever a cocktail includes fruit juice, it always tastes better if the juice is freshly squeezed. Juice from a bottle or carton is better than nothing and the cocktail will still taste good.

Put some crushed ice into a cocktail shaker and pour in the tequila, rum, pineapple juice, grapefruit juice and coconut milk. Shake until a frost forms, then pour into a hurricane glass and decorate with a pineapple wedge. Serve with straws.

Serves 1

Virginia Mint Julep

9 young mint sprigs
1 teaspoon sugar syrup
    (see page 7)
crushed ice
3 measures Bourbon
    whiskey
mint sprig, to decorate

Making the perfect julep is time-consuming. Ideally it should be served in a chilled silver mug. Only crushed ice should be used and the mug mustn't be touched during the preparation, otherwise the frost will disappear. If you haven't got a silver mug, use a tall glass instead.

Put the mint sprigs into an iced silver mug or tall glass. Add the sugar syrup, then crush the mint into the syrup using a teaspoon. Fill the mug or a glass with dry crushed ice, pour the whiskey over the ice and stir until a frost forms. Wrap the mug or glass in a table napkin and serve decorated with a mint sprig.

Serves 1

Stormy Weather

3 ice cubes, cracked
1½ measures gin
¼ measure Mandarine
    Napoléon liqueur
¼ measure dry vermouth
¼ measure sweet
    vermouth
orange rind spiral, to
    decorate

**Mandarine Napoléon is a
French tangerine-flavoured
liqueur.**

Put the ice cubes into a cocktail
shaker and add the gin,
Mandarine Napoléon and dry and
sweet vermouths. Shake to mix
and strain into a chilled cocktail
glass. Decorate the rim of the
glass with the spiral of orange.

Serves 1

exotic associations

St Lucia

4–5 ice cubes
1 measure Curaçao
1 measure dry vermouth
juice of ½ orange
1 teaspoon grenadine
2 measures white or
    golden rum

to decorate
orange rind spiral
cocktail cherry

Put the ice cubes into a cocktail shaker. Pour the Curaçao, dry vermouth, orange juice, grenadine and rum over the ice. Shake until a frost forms, then pour, without straining, into a highball glass. Decorate with an orange rind spiral and a cocktail cherry.

Serves 1

Albemarle Fizz

4–6 ice cubes
1 measure gin
juice of ½ lemon
2 dashes raspberry syrup
½ teaspoon sugar syrup
    (see page 7)
soda water
cocktail cherries, to
    decorate

Put 2–3 ice cubes into a mixing glass and add the gin, lemon juice, raspberry syrup and sugar syrup. Stir to mix then strain into a highball glass. Add 2–3 fresh ice cubes and top up with soda water. Decorate with two cherries on a cocktail stick and serve with straws.

Serves 1

Decatini

ice cubes
2 measures raspberry
   vodka
1 measure morello
   cherry purée
½ measure chocolate
   syrup
½ measure double cream

The combination of raspberry vodka, cherry purée, chocolate syrup and double cream make a splendid cocktail rather like a liquid slice of Black Forest gateau.

Fill a cocktail shaker with ice cubes and add the vodka, chocolate syrup and half of the cream. Shake well and strain into a chilled Martini glass. Shake the cherry purée with the rest of the cream in a clean shaker. Slowly pour the cherry liquid on to a spoon that is held in contact with the chocolate liquid in the glass; this will produce a layering effect. Decorate with a 'swirl' of chocolate syrup.

Paradise

3 ice cubes, cracked
1 dash fresh lemon juice
½ measure fresh orange
    juice
1 measure gin
½ measure apricot brandy
orange and lemon slices,
    to decorate

Put the ice cubes into a cocktail shaker. Add the lemon juice, orange juice, gin and apricot brandy and shake well. Strain into a chilled cocktail glass and decorate with orange and lemon slices.

Serves 1

Party Cocktails

Frozen Pineapple Daiquiri

crushed ice
2–3 pineapple slices
½ measure fresh lime
    juice
1 measure white rum
¼ measure Cointreau
1 teaspoon sugar syrup
    (see page 7)
piece of pineapple,
    to decorate

Put some crushed ice into a blender and add the pineapple slices, lime juice, white rum, Cointreau and sugar syrup. Blend at the highest speed until smooth, then pour into a chilled cocktail glass. Decorate with a piece of fresh pineapple and serve with straw.

Serves 1

Bellini-tini

2 measures vodka
½ measure peach
   schnapps
2 teaspoons peach juice
Champagne
peach slices, to decorate

Pour the vodka, peach schnapps and peach juice into a cocktail shaker and shake thoroughly. Pour into a cocktail glass and top up with Champagne. Decorate with the peach slices.

Serves 1

Tip

Use a juicer to make fresh peach juice or, for small quantities, a citrus squeezer could be used.

Mike Collins

5–6 ice cubes
juice of 1 lemon
1 tablespoon sugar syrup
    (see page 7)
3 measures Irish whiskey
1 orange slice
1 cocktail cherry
soda water
orange rind spiral, to
    decorate

This is a young member of the Collins family of cocktails, of which John or, sometimes, Tom – a gin-based drink – was the first. There are others, too. Pierre Collins is brandy based and Pedro Collins is made with rum. This Irish whiskey version is sometimes called a Mick Collins.

Put the ice cubes into a cocktail shaker. Pour the lemon juice, sugar syrup and whiskey over the ice and shake until a frost forms. Pour, without straining, into a tumbler or Collins glass and add the orange slice and cocktail cherry speared on a cocktail stick. Top up with soda water, stir lightly and serve decorated with an orange rind spiral.

Alexander Baby

4–5 ice cubes
2 measures dark rum
1 measure crème
    de cacao
½ measure double cream
grated nutmeg,
    to decorate

This is the younger – but no less powerful – brother of the classic gin- and brandy-based cocktails, Alexander and Brandy Alexander.

Put the ice cubes into a cocktail shaker and pour the rum, crème de cacao and cream over them. Shake until a frost forms, then strain into a chilled cocktail glass. Sprinkle grated nutmeg on top.

Serves 1

Tropical Dream

1 measure white rum

1 measure Midori

1 tablespoon coconut
    cream

1 tablespoon
    pineapple juice

3 tablespoons fresh
    orange juice

3–4 ice cubes

½ measure crème de
    banane

½ fresh banana

wedge of fresh banana,
    with skin on,
    to decorate

Pour the white rum, Midori,
coconut cream, pineapple juice,
orange juice and the ice cubes
into a blender. Blend for about
10 seconds. Add the crème de
banane and the fresh banana and
blend for a further 10 seconds.
Decorate with the wedge of
banana and drink with a straw.

Serves 1

Crossbow

4–5 ice cubes
½ measure gin
½ measure crème de
    cacao
½ measure Cointreau
drinking chocolate
    powder, to decorate

Chocolate and orange are a classic combination, so créme de cacao and Cointreau form a fantastic partnership to flavour this gin-based cocktail.

Put the ice cubes into a cocktail shaker and add the gin, crème de cacao and Cointreau. Dampen the rim of a chilled cocktail glass with a little water then dip the rim into a saucer of drinking chocolate. Shake the drink vigorously then strain into the prepared glass.

Serves 1

Gin Sling

4–5 ice cubes
juice of ½ lemon
1 measure cherry brandy
3 measures gin
soda water
cherries, to decorate
(optional)

Cherry brandy is a liqueur that is made from macerating cherries in brandy, not distilling brandy from cherries.

Put the ice cubes into a cocktail shaker. Pour the lemon juice, cherry brandy and gin over the ice and shake until a frost forms. Pour without straining into a hurricane glass and top up with soda water. Decorate with cherries, if liked, and serve with straws.

Serves 1

Celebration Cocktail

1 lemon wedge
caster sugar
3 ice cubes
1 measure brandy
1 dash Bénédictine
1 dash crème de mure
Champagne

Frost the rim of a Champagne flute with the lemon wedge and sugar. Put the ice into a cocktail shaker and add the brandy, Bénédictine and crème de mure. Shake well, strain into the flute and top up with Champagne.

Serves 1

Benedict

3–4 ice cubes
1 measure Bénédictine
3 measures Scotch
    whisky
dry ginger ale

Bénédictine is a world-famous liqueur that has been produced by Bénédictine monks since the early 16th century. It is flavoured with aromatic herbs and spices according to a secret recipe.

Put the ice cubes into a mixing glass. Pour the Bénédictine and whisky over the ice. Stir evenly without splashing and, without straining, pour the cocktail into a chilled highball glass. Top up with dry ginger ale and serve.

Serves 1

Texas Tea

¾ measure tequila
1 tablespoon white rum
1 tablespoon Cointreau
2 teaspoons sugar syrup
  (see page 7)
¾ measure fresh
  lemon juice
¾ measure fresh
  orange juice
100 ml (3½ fl oz) strong
  fruit tea, chilled
ice cubes

to decorate
orange slice
lemon slice
mint sprig

Pour the tequila, rum, Cointreau, sugar syrup, lemon juice, orange juice and tea into a cocktail shaker, add a handful of ice cubes and shake vigorously. Fill a 350 ml (12 fl oz) sling glass with fresh ice cubes and strain the drink over them. Decorate with orange and lemon slices and a mint sprig.

Serves 1

Tip

One of the best teas to use as a base for this refreshing drink is a mixed berry tea. Its essential fruitiness blends very well with the citrus juices in Texas Tea.

Coco-oco

crushed ice

4 teaspoons creamed
    coconut or coconut
    syrup

2 teaspoons fresh lemon
    juice

1 teaspoon maraschino
    syrup

100 ml (3½ fl oz) full-fat
    milk

4 dashes Angostura
    bitters

to decorate
pineapple leaf
pineapple wedge
cocktail cherry

Put the ice into a food processor
and add the creamed coconut or
coconut syrup, lemon juice,
maraschino syrup, milk and
bitters. Process for a few
seconds. Pour into a tall glass
and decorate with a pineapple
leaf, a pineapple wedge and a
cocktail cherry. Serve with
a straw.

Serves 1

Honeymoon

crushed ice
1 measure maple syrup
   or clear honey
4 teaspoons fresh lime
   juice
1 measure fresh orange
   juice
1 measure apple juice
cocktail cherry,
   to decorate

Put some crushed ice into a cocktail shaker and add the maple syrup or honey, lime juice, orange juice and apple juice. Shake well then strain into a chilled cocktail glass. Decorate with a cherry on a cocktail stick.

Serves 1

Cool Passion

500 ml (17 fl oz) orange
    and passion fruit juice
1 litre (1¾ pints)
    pineapple juice
1.5 litres (2½ pints)
    lemonade
crushed ice

to decorate
blackberries
mint sprigs

Pour the two fruit juices into
a large jug. Stir well to mix.
Just before serving, stir in the
lemonade. Pour into glasses
containing crushed ice and
decorate each one with a
blackberry and mint sprig.

Serves 20

Midsummer Punch

125 g (4 oz) sugar
300 ml (½ pint) water
300 ml (½ pint) fresh
     orange juice
300 ml (½ pint) pineapple
     juice
600 ml (1 pint) cold weak
     tea, strained
orange, lemon, apple and
     pineapple slices
crushed ice
300 ml (½ pint) ginger ale
mint sprigs, to decorate

Put the sugar and water into a saucepan and stir over a low heat until the sugar has dissolved. Leave to cool, then pour into a large jug or bowl. Stir in the fruit juices and cold tea, then add the sliced fruit and the crushed ice. To serve, pour into tall glasses and top up with ginger ale. Decorate with mint sprigs.

Serves 8–10

San Francisco

3 ice cubes
1 measure fresh orange
   juice
1 measure fresh lemon
   juice
1 measure pineapple
   juice
1 measure fresh
   grapefruit juice
2 dashes grenadine
1 egg white
soda water

Put the ice cubes into a cocktail shaker and pour in the orange, lemon, pineapple and grapefruit juices, grenadine and egg white. Shake well then strain into a large goblet. Top up with soda water and decorate with the lemon and lime slices, a cocktail cherry on a cocktail stick and an orange spiral. Serve with a straw.

Serves 1

to decorate
lemon slice
lime slice
cocktail cherry
orange spiral

INDEX

NEW PHOTOGRAPHY
by Stephen Conroy
Cocktails styled by
David Morgan

**ACKNOWLEDGEMENTS
IN SOURCE ORDER**
Little Book of Exotic
Cocktails

**Octopus Publishing
Group Limited**/Jean Cazals
5, 43/Stephen Conroy 2, 3,
6-7, 8, 21, 26, 29, 31, 50,
53, 67, 69, 70, 75, 79, 83,
89, 93/Neil Mersh 11, 47,
55, 63, 81, 95/William
Reavell 13, 15, 17, 18, 22,
25, 32, 35, 37, 39, 41, 45,
49, 56, 59, 61, 65, 73, 77,
84, 87, 91